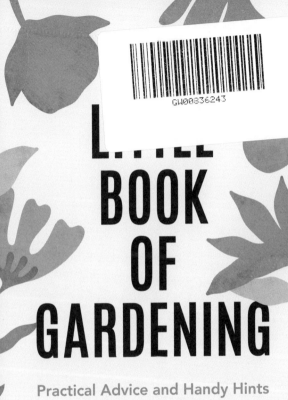

LITTLE BOOK OF GARDENING

Practical Advice and Handy Hints for Aspiring Gardeners

Simon Zonenblick

summersdale

An Hachette UK Company
www.hachette.co.uk

Summersdale Publishers
Part of Octopus Publishing Group Limited
Carmelite House
50 Victoria Embankment
LONDON
EC4Y 0DZ
UK

www.summersdale.com

This FSC® label means that materials used for the product have been responsibly sourced

MIX
Paper | Supporting responsible forestry
FSC® C018236
www.fsc.org

The authorized representative in the EEA is Hachette Ireland, 8 Castlecourt Centre, Dublin 15, D15 XTP3, Ireland (email: info@hbgi.ie)

Printed and bound in Poland

ISBN: 978-1-83799-547-9

CONTENTS

Introduction / **04**

Chapter One:
Gardening Essentials / **07**

Chapter Two:
An Identification Guide / **42**

Chapter Three:
Landscaping Ideas / **79**

Farewell / **125**

Index / **126**

INTRODUCTION

We are gardening more than ever. According to surveys, more than half the population in America and Europe are getting green-fingered, and data shows that numbers are rising.

Humans have been creating gardens for thousands of years. The cultivation of plants emerged around 12,000 years ago in the context of agriculture and producing food. In many ancient civilizations, rich and powerful people chose to pursue it for aesthetic purposes, with Egyptian tomb paintings providing evidence of ornamental horticulture, including lotus ponds and "pleasure gardens", full of palm trees, acacias, tamarisk and willows. The Persians, Greeks and Romans were renowned for their beautiful gardens, and the Hanging Gardens of Babylon were among the Wonders of the Ancient World.

Throughout history, there have been many innovative styles of gardening, reflecting different cultural values and aesthetics. In China and Japan, gardens often expressed a balanced relationship with nature, skilfully blending rocks, water and ornamental plants. In contrast, the grand gardens of Renaissance and Baroque Europe emphasized grandeur and formal design.

By the nineteenth century, British landowners commonly employed designers such as Capability Brown to craft vast landscapes. More recently, as modern housing made gardens accessible to more people, "cottage gardens" enabled naturalistic displays in confined spaces.

Gardening offers a great antidote to the pace of modern life, providing benefits for physical, mental and emotional well-being. Many people find gardening helps them feel connected to nature, with the simple acts of watering, digging and pruning providing physical and mental benefits. The soothing melodies of birds and bees, and the rustling of leaves in the breeze enhance the sense of relaxation, making gardening a truly restorative activity.

As our awareness of the plight of the planet grows, gardening has become an excellent way to support biodiversity. Eco-friendly practices are regaining prominence, making it easier to garden in ways that not only minimize harm, but often have positive impacts on the environment. In *The Little Book of Gardening*, we will celebrate these sustainable methods and explore how gardening can help us welcome the wild into our own habitats.

The information in these pages will also help tailor your gardening activities to suit your lifestyle and location, offering new ideas and tips, along with some tried-and-tested favourites. You will be guided through the basics of choosing tools and plants, the terminology of gardening, and a few horticultural dos and don'ts. You'll also find advice on planning a garden, managing pests and diseases, and dealing with unpredictable weather.

Whether you're a beginner looking to develop your skills, expanding your existing knowledge, tackling a large-scale project or getting started in a small yard, *The Little Book of Gardening* is the ideal companion. It will help you garden at your own pace, in your own time and in your own way.

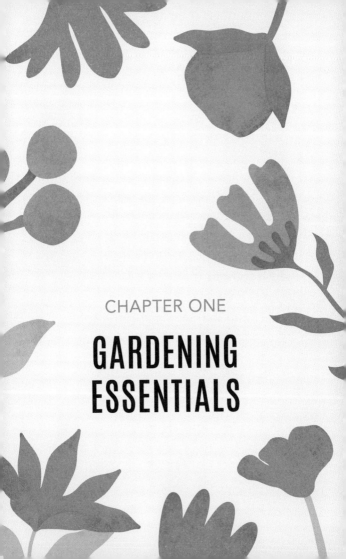

CHAPTER ONE

GARDENING ESSENTIALS

In this chapter, we'll explore some of the essential equipment needed to maintain any garden, whether large or small. From versatile tools that make everyday tasks easier to specialized items for specific needs, having the right gear can make all the difference. You'll also find a handy list of dos and don'ts, some troubleshooting tips, and important precautions to keep in mind. So first, let's take a look at some of the tools every gardener should have.

GARDENING TOOLS

Spade

Garden spades come in many shapes and sizes. A good spade should have a balanced weight, a long, sturdy shaft, and a comfortable, secure grip. Lighter spades with wider handles are easier to manage, and placing your foot on the head for added leverage should feel comfortable.

Tilted handles are ideal for shallow digging, while spades made from a single block of forged steel are better suited for deep digging and tackling tough soils or overgrown roots. Curved heads suit sandy, loose soils whereas heavy soils like clay may require square-point spades or shovels.

Hoe

Used a bit like a brush, hoes are great for severing dead plants or rubbish or tilling and cultivating soil. Their small heads provide for close shaping of soils, and they are an effective way of loosening earth.

Digging fork

Digging forks are ideal for turning soil and breaking up thick, tangled roots. Some gardeners use two forks placed back-to-back to separate stubborn clumps of roots. The prongs or "tines" are thinner than the heads of spades or hoes, allowing them to penetrate deeply into the ground or dislodge stones without severing roots as a long blade might.

 # Trowel

A trowel is invaluable for weeding, transplanting and close-up digging. It should feel comfortable to grip, with a good weight balance between handle and head. For heavier, deeper digging, stainless-steel blades are ideal, while lighter jobs, like digging holes for small plants or aerating soil, are easier with trowels that have lightweight aluminium heads. Increasingly, garden trowels are being made with composite materials like fibreglass, offering a blend of durability and lightness.

 # Secateurs

Secateurs are essential for pruning, deadheading, cutting back and snipping off unwanted twigs and growth. There are three main types:

🌼 **Anvil:** These act like knives against blocks, enabling sharp, clean cuts. Suitable for cutting through thick stems and dead wood.

🌼 **Bypass:** With two blades that bypass each other like scissors, these secateurs are suitable for fresh, soft growth. To maintain their effectiveness, the blades should be kept sharp using methods like sandpaper, wool scouring pads or sharpening stones.

🌼 **Ratchet:** These have anvil or bypass blades, but also include ratchet springs, making it possible to chop or prune in gradual cuts. This design is particularly useful for cutting wood or stems, especially for gardeners with limited hand strength or those recovering from injury, as it requires repeated squeezing and releasing of the handles.

Loppers

Similar to secateurs, loppers are available in anvil, bypass or ratchet forms, but they are mostly used for pruning trees, tall bushes and shrubs. Unlike secateurs, loppers have long handles and large blades, providing greater leverage and cutting power. Some models also feature levers to increase cutting force.

Shears

Shorter than loppers, garden shears are handy for pruning thick shrubs and branches, or snipping hedges. Their long handles make it easier to cut at different angles, and they come in both anvil and bypass types. Lightweight shears with durable handles and steel blades are the easiest to use and provide clean, precise cuts. Shears designed for hedge or grass cutting feature long, narrow blades, while those intended for delicate plants like roses have smaller, sharper blades. Lawn edging shears are distinct, with blades set at a sharp right angle to the handles, often reinforced with chrome for added toughness.

 # Rake

Rakes are essentially brooms for the garden, with tines or "teeth" that effectively gather and remove leaves from grass, making them invaluable for tidying up lawns. Rakes come in wood, metal or plastic form. Rakes with extendable shafts are useful for easy transportation and storage.

 # Lawn mower

Lawn mowers come in many variations, ranging from electric and cordless models to non-motorized "push" mowers. For smaller yards and gardens, push mowers are often ideal, while electric self-propelling mowers are better suited for larger spaces. Many modern mowers are designed to be lightweight and offer additional features like adjustable cutting heights. When choosing a mower, it's worth researching the options on the market and considering factors such as horsepower, cutting width and fuel type.

Watering can or hose

While many gardeners let rainfall take care of much of their garden's water needs, a good watering can is still essential. It's often helpful to have several cans in different sizes. Small, long-spouted cans with upright handles are perfect for precise watering of seedlings and individual plants in rockeries or small plots. Larger, more capacious cans are ideal for watering clumps of plants and borders, without needing to refill frequently.

When selecting a watering can, consider factors like durability – will it crack if dropped on concrete? – and spout reach – will you be watering amid dense foliage? Value and comfort are also important, especially if you'll be using it for extended periods. Some gardeners avoid open-topped cans, which can cause splashes, while others like cans with two spouts, providing different pouring options. Cans with alterable spouts or nozzles allow you to flip between modes of pouring, such as spray and sprinkle.

A garden hose should be chosen on the basis of need. For example, sprinkler or soak hoses are designed for plants or lawns – they have perforated sides which spray or leak water into the air or allow it to trickle into the soil. Rubber hoses are ultra-durable, while a vinyl hose makes for easy handling. Most gardeners prefer brass nozzles for minimizing leaks. Modern garden hoses often come in kits, complete with accessories like extenders, valves, soakers, splitters and adaptors for multiple spray options.

An eco-friendly, cost-effective take on watering equipment is the water butt – a container for storing rainwater. This is excellent for conserving water, reducing tap water use and saving on your water bill, especially during dry weather or hosepipe bans. Rainwater is rich in organic matter and nitrates, slightly acidic, and free from chemicals like chlorine.

If a shop-bought water butt is not an option, try storing water in plastic containers, thus adding an element of recycling into your gardening.

Other equipment

Other items that make gardening easier include **kneeling pads**, or "kneelers", which take the strain off your knees, joints and back. These pads make it easier to grapple with ground-based tasks without crouching. Most garden centres sell kneelers with foam cores which conform to the shape of your knees. Alternatively, you can create your own kneelers by stuffing old pairs of jeans with fabric scraps and stitching the ends – a great way to make gardening more comfortable while embracing a zero-waste approach.

A **wheelbarrow** is a superb way of transporting materials such as soil and compost, or leaves for composting.

Garden twine, along with **stakes** or **canes**, is invaluable for tying plants that need support, like tomatoes, or marking spaces for planting in rows.

Cloches act as mini greenhouses protecting plants from frost or pests, while a **cold frame** is used for similar purposes, but tends to be kept over plants for extended periods. You can make your own cold frame out of bricks and glass.

Dibbers make holes in the soil for sowing seeds, transplanting seedlings or planting bulbs. A **pH testing kit** reveals the pH (acid/alkaline) levels of your garden's soil, which can be useful for selecting appropriate plants.

A **knife** can be useful for tasks like weeding and dividing, measuring soil depth, or mapping out rows for planting. Gardening knives come in various forms, the most popular being the "patio knife", whose thin blades are designed for weeding between paving stones, while the budding knife is used for more delicate tasks. For maintaining larger features like hedges, tools like **hedge trimmers** or **edgers**, typically electric, are essential.

Finally, while many gardeners like to feel the soil beneath their fingernails, a good pair of **gloves** is a must-have, even as a "just in case". For everyday gardening tasks like planting and pruning, thin, light gloves provide adequate protection against prickles and dirt. For more demanding landscaping jobs, more heavy-duty gloves may be required.

Now that we've considered the vital tools of gardening, let's explore some common gardening terminology.

GARDENING GLOSSARY

Use this gardener's glossary, split into three sections, to familiarize yourself with terms and phrases you may come across.

 ## Associated with plants and their biology

Annual – A plant that completes its life cycle (from seed germination, through flowering and fruiting, to death) in one season.

Anther – Pollen-bearing part of the stamen.

Apical bud – Primary growth point located at the tip of a stem, where new growth originates.

Basal – The area at or close to the base of a plant, typically in relation to foliage.

Biennial – A plant with a life cycle of two seasons.

Bract – Leaf-like structure that often supports or surrounds a flower.

Bud – Embryonic shoot, usually seen at the stem tip or leaf axils.

Bulb – Short underground storage organ in the form of a stem with fleshy leaf bases called scales.

Corolla – Collective name for the petals of a flower.

Creeper – Plant with a trailing growth habit that climbs across or up surfaces using tendrils or aerial roots.

Deciduous – Plants that shed their leaves at the end of the growing season, renewing them at the beginning of the next.

Evergreen – Plants that retain their leaves throughout the year.

Family – A major grouping of plants, useful for bracketing genera (see below) that share common features. The largest family is the *Asteraceae* (compound plants), which includes the daisies and contains 1,550 genera and 26,000 species.

Foliage – The leaves of a plant.

Genera/genus – Groupings of plant species within families. The genus name is capitalized and followed by the species name, e.g. *Rosa gallica* (Gallic rose).

Germination – Process whereby a plant grows from a seed or spores, resulting in a small plant or seedling (known collectively as "new shoots").

Hardy – A plant that can live through low temperatures. Some plants can be described as frost-hardy, or half-hardy (survive moderately low temperatures or light frost).

Hybrid – A plant formed by pollination between two varieties.

Inflorescence – A cluster or arrangement of flower heads on a plant.

Panicle – A type of inflorescence with many branches.

Pedicel – Structure which connects an inflorescence to the stem.

Perennial – A plant whose life cycle lasts at least three years.

Petals – Modified leaves surrounding a flower's reproductive parts, often brightly coloured and usually attractive to pollinators.

Photosynthesis – The process by which plants, algae and some bacteria harness light energy to convert carbon dioxide (CO_2) and water (H_2O) into oxygen. The chemical reaction generates carbohydrates, which the plant consumes, and releases oxygen needed by living things to breathe. Photosynthesis takes place within the chloroplasts, which give leaves their green colour.

Pollen – Powdery substance produced by many plants, which is essential for reproduction.

Prickle – Sharp projection on a plant, often serving as a deterrent to predators.

Raceme – An unbranched stem bearing flowers with short stalks along its axis.

Rhizome – Thick underground stem.

Roots – Organs that anchor a plant and take in water and nutrients from the soil, typically located underground.

Sepals – Green, petal-like parts of a flower, usually arranged below the petals and protecting the flower in bud.

Shoot – New plant growth, often referring to stems, leaves or buds.

Species – Grouping of plants within a genus. In plant classification, the species name follows the genus name and is not capitalized, e.g. *Narcissus poeticus*.

Spike – An inflorescence where flowers are attached directly to the stem without pedicels.

Stamen – Pollen-producing male organ of a flower.

Stem – The main axis of a plant, supporting the flowers, foliage and fruits, and transporting water and nutrients.

Stigma – The part of a flower that receives pollen, usually from pollinating birds or insects, or by hand.

Style – Organ connecting stigma to ovary.

Thorn – Stiff and woody modified stem with a hard point, usually at the ends of stems or branchlets.

Tuber – An enlarged underground storage organ providing nutrients during winter or dry months.

Umbel – A flower cluster on short spreading stems that come from the same point.

Variegated – Differing colouring or patterns on leaves.

Variety – Variation within a species formed naturally in the plant's native environment.

Vector – Organism, typically an insect, spreading disease to plants.

Volunteer – Self-seeded plant that grows without being intentionally planted.

Gardening and
botanical activities

Aeration – Introduction of air and oxygen into soil, enhancing oxygen availability to roots and beneficial micro-organisms.

Companion planting – Growing combinations of plants to provide mutual benefits, including attracting pollinators, deterring pests, encouraging healthy growth and providing shade.

Composting – Adding decomposed organic waste to the soil to improve structure, fertility, aeration and biodiversity.

Crop rotation – Introducing and growing different crops in the same area across different years or seasons, reducing the depletion of nutrients due to over-reliance, and reducing the activity of pests by preventing them from over-adapting to the plants.

Deadheading – Removing dead or fading flowers to encourage more blooms.

Division – Splitting up a plant, often one formed in multiple clumps, into sections to be re-planted and grown as individual plants.

Frost date – Average first or last date your area receives frost.

Full sun – A location that receives at least 6 hours of sunlight per day.

Green manure – Crops worked into soil for composting purposes before decomposition, such as leaves, stems and twigs.

Hardening off – Gradually acclimating plants, often seedlings or those kept indoors, to the outdoor climate by moving them outside for increasing amounts of time each day.

Mulching – Materials such as compost, leaves or grass, placed onto soil around the edges of plants, to protect from predators, retain soil moisture and prevent or limit weed growth and soil erosion.

Organic gardening – Cultivating plants without pesticides and chemicals.

Pinching out – Removing a plant's main stem to encourage the growth of two new stems below the cut.

Planting – Placing of the plant in the part of the garden where it is going to grow, usually from a pot or container, or from a greenhouse. Involves preparing soil, firming up soil around the base of the plant once planted, and "watering in".

Pot bound/root bound – When a plant's roots are crowded into a ball shape in its pot/container, causing wilting and stunted growth, potentially killing the plant.

Potting up/re-potting – The process of transferring plants from smaller pots or seed trays into larger containers or pots to accommodate growth.

Propagation – The natural or artificial process of growing new plants.

Pruning – Selectively cutting stems and branches to promote better plant health, reducing disease and removing spent flowers.

Self-seeding – Plants which produce seeds that fall directly into the soil to germinate in that location.

Sowing – The act of planting seeds, usually by spreading over soil or growing matter.

Thinning – Removal of flowers, shoots and seedlings to provide space and aeration for others.

Transplanting – Removal of a plant from one growing situation to another, usually from a pot to a larger container or directly into the ground.

Weeding – Removal of unwanted plants from a garden or specific area.

Common garden features

Border – Landscaping feature creating a separated space with rows of plants, typically arranged around the edges of a garden. Floral borders often frame the garden and define its boundaries.

Cold frame – Structure with a transparent top, used to protect plants from frost and extend the growing season.

Flower bed – Any area of land where flowers are purposely grown.

pH – Balance or measure of alkalinity and acidity in soil. The pH scale ranges from 0 (highly acidic) to 14 (high alkalinity) with 7 being neutral.

Pollinator – An organism, such as a bird or a bee, that transfers pollen from the anther of a plant to the stigma of another.

Raised bed – Platform with soil raised above ground, often enclosed by wood or blocks. Growing in this way minimizes weed growth and reduces reliance on poor native soils. Since gardeners do not step on raised beds, the risk of treading on plants is reduced.

Rockery – Area of a garden, often raised, where the gardener lays out stones and rocks, and plants around them.

Trellis – Frame-like structure used for supporting climbing plants, often composed in lattice-like arrangements, and made of wood, metal or bamboo.

Water feature – A garden feature, such as a pond or fountain, that provides visual focus or attracts wildlife and can be used to grow aquatic plants.

DOS AND DON'TS OF GARDENING

All gardeners have their own tricks of the trade, and what works for your friend or neighbour may not be ideal for your purposes. However, various techniques have passed the test of time, and are worth bearing in mind, regardless of the size or style of your garden or what you choose to grow. Equally, there are common mistakes all gardeners should avoid. Let's cast an eye over some of these tried-and-true methods along with the pitfalls to steer clear of.

 Ten gardening dos

1. **Do** familiarize yourself with the needs of the plants you wish to cultivate.

2. **Do** familiarize yourself with the environment you are working with – its climate, which wildlife thrives there and which plants are more likely to succeed. Consider the physical situation of your garden, such as its exposure to wind, light or shade.

3. **Do** grow plants in conditions they naturally thrive in.

4. **Do** provide space for plants to grow and seeds to germinate.

5. **Do** think long term – are your plants likely to produce large blooms that will outgrow the available space? How will each plant look alongside the others you are cultivating?

6. **Do** prune at optimum times. Pruning promotes new growth and is vital to the healthy maintenance of garden plants, but if done too early or too late can result in weakened or damaged plants.

7. **Do** remove dead, diseased or overcrowded plants. This helps prevent unnecessary competition for nutrients and ensures higher chances of survival for the plants you want to grow.

8. **Do** wear the correct protective equipment when operating machinery.

9. **Do** keep tools clean between use. This maximizes effectiveness and minimizes damage and need for replacement.

10. **Do** find a pattern of gardening that suits you. A garden that suits your interests, such as a wildlife or vegetable garden, with requirements suited to your schedule, will be easier to maintain.

Ten gardening don'ts

1. **Don't** plant without preparing the soil, and preferably testing its content. Measuring the space to be used, and adding fertilizers, composts or manures ensures their new environments are as conducive to the healthy development of your plants as possible.

2. **Don't** plant at the wrong time of year. Most plants from garden centres, nurseries and shops come with information tags advising the best times for planting, or these can be sourced via the internet or books.

3. **Don't** waste water by watering in heavy sun (often mid-afternoon), when it will quickly dry up. Plants prefer being watered in the morning or evening, when temperatures are cooler and water can run down to the roots with less evaporation.

4. **Don't** under-water. Too little water starves a plant's roots and results in wilting, discolouring of leaves and vulnerability to pests.

5. **Don't** overwater. Excessive watering interferes with gases, reducing oxygen supplies to the roots.

6. **Don't** apply liquid fertilizers directly onto plants or seeds, which can cause burning. Dilute with water and apply from a few inches back.

7. **Don't** work soil immediately after heavy rain. Wait until it is drier to avoid disturbing its structure.

8. **Don't** dig near roots as this can kill or damage them.

9. **Don't** use chemical pesticides harmful to ecology and wildlife if you can avoid them.

10. **Don't** endanger wildlife with features like netting. If investing in these, research responsible use.

TROUBLESHOOTING

Gardening comes with its fair share of challenges, from pests and diseases to unpredictable weather. Below you'll find some effective ways to tackle these obstacles.

 ## Pests

While pests are a frequent problem for most gardeners, non-toxic, biological controls are increasingly preferred over those which involve the use of chemicals. If you learn which predators prey on particular pests and attract them with your planting, you can limit pest activity while also helping nature. For example, you can encourage frogs (which eat slugs) with water features, or birds like thrushes (which like to feast on snails) with food such as sunflower seeds placed on a table. Prevention is key, so it is worth discovering what is attracting the pests in the first place. You might consider avoiding certain plants or neighbouring them with "trap crops" (see "Green Fingers" section in Kitchen Gardening, Chapter Three). Mulches can also provide a barrier around the stems, while coffee grounds or copper strips deter slugs and snails.

Diseases

Research diseases that may affect your plants and monitor for symptoms. Clean and disinfect tools before and after use, select disease-resistant plant varieties, and water plants from below via drip irrigation systems where possible, to suppress conditions favourable for disease, like humidity around foliage. Although disease management is a big topic, many gardeners find a basic understanding is sufficient. Below is a list of ten common diseases and strategies for managing them:

Bacterial wilt

Plants affected: Mostly *Cucurbitaceae* (squashes, pumpkins, etc.) and *Solanaceae* (common bean and tomato) genera.

Causes: Pathogens spread by striped cucumber beetles (*Acalymma vittatum*) and spotted cucumber beetles (*Diabrotica undecimpunctata*).

Symptoms: Wilting of individual leaves, soon whole stem.

Effects: Blockage of water transportation in stems.

Preventions: Reduce beetle access by crop rotation, planting on raised beds and maintaining plant health (vectors are attracted to plants with existing wilt).

Camellia flower blight

Plants affected: *Camellia* species.

Causes: Fungus entering through pruning cuts, damage or natural openings.

Symptoms: Spots on leaves and flowers. Flowers turn brown and mushy before falling off.

Effects: Damage to flower tissue with eventual plant collapse.

Preventions: The fungus thrives in moisture on foliage and flowers, so water plants at bases. Remove affected foliage or flowers. A fungicide spray may be needed once infected.

Cankers

Plants affected: *Prunus* genus that includes cherries, plums and apricots.

Causes: Fungus.

Symptoms: Oval areas of dead, sunken bark, often with flaky dead bark covering affected area. Additional signs include leaf holes ("shotholes") and a colourful, gummy growth called gummosis forming on the bark.

Effects: Branches and fruit affected will weaken and die. *Prunus* shoots affected by bacterial cankers may fail to fully emerge or die back.

Preventions: Cankers are thought to be worse on wet, heavy or acid soils, so ensure good drainage. Soil levels can be increased with added lime. Prevent bacterial cankers by pruning in July or August when tissues are most disease resistant.

Cures: Branches and infected bark should be cut out or cut back to green tissue. Apply protective wood paint to cut area to prevent re-infection.

Cucumber mosaic virus

Plants affected: Though first found in cucumbers, the virus affects many vegetables including aubergines, beans, beets, carrots, celery, lettuce, melons, peppers, spinach, squashes, tomatoes and some non-culinary plants including daffodils, delphiniums, lilies, primroses, and more.

Causes: Plant virus spread by aphids.

Symptoms: Yellow mottling and distorted growth of foliage. White streaks on flowers.

Effects: Stunted growth, distorted fruit and reduced yields.

Preventions: Avoid handling plants after coming into contact with the infection until you have thoroughly washed your hands and disinfected tools. Be aware that groundsel and chickweed are known to harbour the virus.

Downy mildew

Plants affected: Wide varieties of both edible and ornamental plants.

Causes: Parasitic microbes.

Symptoms: Yellow areas on leaves quickly turning brown.

Effects: Lack of vigour, stunted growth, reduced yields (in fruit plants) and in some cases plant death.

Preventions: Water from below if possible; selective pruning improves air circulation, lessening humidity.

Cures: Remove and destroy affected plants.

Fireblight

Plants affected: Mostly pears but also others in the *Rosaceae* genus.

Causes: Pathogen.

Symptoms: Watery fruits, wilting shoots, blossoms shrivelling, branches blackening and eventually cracking. Bacterial ooze visible in cracks.

Effects: Wilting of blossoms, shrivelling and dying of shoots, temporary staining of bark in a reddish colour, emergence of cankers. Can result in the death of entire orchards.

Preventions: Regular inspection with removal of infected parts.

Grey mould

Plants affected: Many, but most frequent in wine grapes.

Causes: Fungus entering through cuts (can affect healthy plants in humid conditions).

Symptoms: Brown fuzz on affected buds, foliage or flowers.

Effects: Tissue decay causing plants and fruits to shrivel.

Preventions: Remove dead or dying parts. If indoors, reduce vapour and humidity by opening vents to improve ventilation.

Onion white rot

Plants affected: Onions, garlics, leeks.

Causes: Fungus often spread by cross-contamination on allotments.

Symptoms: Foliage yellows and wilts.

Effects: Bulb decay.

Preventions: Watch for symptoms in summer to mid-fall. Avoid contaminating soil with unwashed tools or footwear.

Powdery mildew

Plants affected: Wide variety. Species will tend to be affected by their own specific type of powdery mildew.

Causes: Fungus, spores spread by wind.

Symptoms: White, dusty coating on stems and foliage.

Effects: Discolouration and possible distortion of foliage.

Preventions: Reduce humidity with adequately spaced planting and pruning. Removing infected shoots reduces chances of further infection.

Rusts

Plants affected: Rusts can affect many different plants both edible and ornamental.

Causes: Fungal disease whereby spores land on host plants.

Symptoms: Pale leaf spots which develop into masses of orange, yellow, white, black or brown spores or "pustules", which can reach up to dozens per leaf and can occasionally also appear on stems, flowers and fruits.

Effects: Can reduce plant vigour and cause stunted growth or yellowing, and in extreme cases (as with *Antirrhinum* rusts) death.

Preventions: Good garden hygiene and avoiding excessive liquid nitrogen fertilizer (which creates soft lush growth prone to rusts) help ward off the risks, while individual affected leaves may be removed by hand if small in number (removing large numbers of leaves may cause more harm). Organic solutions like sulphur powder can stop the germination of spores. Organic fungicides might be considered but some can have harmful environmental effects. Leaving diseased plant parts above ground, or in compost, will cause further spread; dispose of them by burning responsibly or as garden waste at the tip.

 Weeds

A weed is a plant, usually a wildflower, in a place you do not want it. Wherever possible, it is good to work with rather than against nature, especially if you are aiming for a wild-looking garden, or for plants to attract pests away from prized crops. Bear in mind that perennial weeds like hedge bindweed, bramble, dandelions and thistles attract pollinators. If you definitely want to remove them, here are a few tips for eliminating weeds:

- ❋ **Remove by roots:** Invasive species are tenacious growers and will re-emerge if root fragments remain in the soil.

- ❋ **Cover weed-prone areas which presumably harbour weed-friendly conditions:** After weeding, cover with light-excluding material such as thick black plastic, weed membrane, compost or leaf mould. This prevents weeds re-emerging especially in areas that may contain root fragments.

- ❋ **Hoe for small weeds:** Hoeing is effective, especially in early stages of growth.

- ❋ **Suppress with ground cover:** Plant ground cover species like creeping thyme, ivy or *Senecio tropaeolifolius* (false nasturtium). These plants also help guard against soil erosion.

 ## Conditions

Knowing your garden's physical situation, soil type and moisture levels will help minimize risks. For instance, if gardening in moisture-retaining soil, consider planting *Berberis stenophylla*, *Lobelia cardinalis* or *Magnolia grandiflora*. Drought-tolerant plants are generally those growing naturally in dry conditions; these include cacti, succulents and other desert plants like bottlebrush and yuccas. For alkaline soil, plants such as *Origanum vulgare* (aureum), *Lonicera periclymenum* (serotina) or *Euonymus europaeus* are good choices. Acid-loving plants include azaleas, heathers and *Zenobia pulverulenta* (dusty zenobia). Many hardy shrubs, ornamental grasses and trees are wind resistant, while those that are less tolerant might do better in the protection of pots.

Remember, you can find plants to suit all seasons. The final days of summer can be brightened by vivid red and orange flowers like those of *Crocosmia*, while snowdrops, crocuses and many primroses are among the winter flowering plants that can keep your garden lively once the summer fades.

Finally, soil terminology can be a bit misleading – "poor soil", for example, is a technical term relating to matters like pH imbalances or nutrient limitations, not unsuitability for growth. Some plants actually prefer poor soil: lavenders thrive with few nutrients, certain periwinkles tolerate clay, and *Buddleja davidii* often flowers on waste ground.

TIPS FOR
SAFE GARDENING

1. Take regular breaks and rotate tasks to avoid repetitive strain injuries.

2. Consider warming-up exercises like slow stretches to prepare your body for physical activity.

3. Maintain good posture while gardening; stretch your back periodically and avoid uncomfortable positions.

4. Avoid contact with chemicals and wash your hands thoroughly if you do handle them.

5. Know which plants are poisonous to humans or animals and learn how to handle them safely.

6. Always wear gloves – they're useful for protecting your hands from cuts, irritants and dirt.

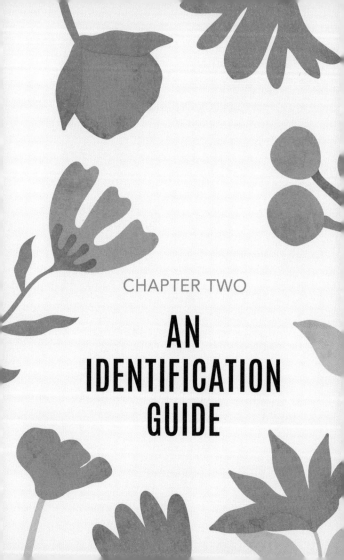

CHAPTER TWO

AN
IDENTIFICATION
GUIDE

Plants can be categorized into many groups, from families and genera to species with male and female parts on the same or separate plants. But the most straightforward division is between perennials, biennials and annuals.

This chapter is split into three parts, featuring 15 popular perennials, 15 beloved annuals and a selection of biennials. The plants showcased offer a diverse array of options to help you plan and develop your garden.

AGAPANTHUS PRAECOX

One of several *Agapanthus* plants known as African lily, *A. praecox* is a clump-forming perennial native to South Africa, whose blue flowers form in umbels.

FAMILY: *Amaryllidaceae*

FLOWERS: Umbels of mostly blue flowers, though they can be purple or white, appear in summer.

LEAVES: Long, strap-like.

HABIT: Herbaceous. Overwinters in stump form (it survives the winter season by reducing itself to a compact, hardened base).

PREFERRED ENVIRONMENT: Well-drained soil in full sun, and can withstand cold and wind – and, once established, short periods of drought.

GROWING TIPS: Plant in early spring. To protect young plants from molluscs, spread handfuls of wood ash around stumps. Mulch will harden them off in frosts and cold temperatures down to −15°C. Does not respond well to transplantation. Propagate by division.

PESTS AND DISEASES: Slugs and snails can be a problem for young shoots.

ARMERIA MARITIMA

Evergreen alpine perennial, pretty pink flowers in late spring and summer. *A. maritima*, commonly called thrift, is a popular rockery plant.

FAMILY: *Plumbaginaceae*

FLOWERS: Typically, tiny pink flowers on long stems.

LEAVES: Basal rosettes of narrow, smooth leaves, surrounding the stalk.

HABIT: Compact, clump forming thrift is a coastal plant, enjoying sandy, dry conditions.

PREFERRED ENVIRONMENT: Well-drained sandy soil in full sun. Seeds can be sown in trays or pots of moist compost and then transplanted to a sunny location.

GROWING TIPS: Plant in spring or early summer. Deadheading faded flowers will promote second blooms. Clumps can grow around 50 cm tall.

PESTS AND DISEASES: Largely disease resistant with no particular pests. Most problems arise from being overwatered or in overly moist soils, which can cause crown and root rot. Nutrient deficiencies may cause leaf rust.

CALLUNA VULGARIS

Bee-attracting, evergreen shrubs native to moors, heaths and alpine environments. Known as heathers, they are hardy and grow well in cold conditions. Cultivated in wide arrays of colours though their familiar mauve shades are popular. With golden foliage, they can bring moorland colour to your garden even in the depths of winter.

FAMILY: *Ericaceae*

FLOWERS: The stems bear pink or mauve flowers with sepal-like basal leaf structures in summer.

LEAVES: 2–3 mm long, oppositely arranged, oval to lanceolate.

HABIT: Compact clumps but in nature forms large blankets of flowers. Ideal for pots.

PREFERRED ENVIRONMENT: Well-drained acidic soils.

GROWING TIPS: Plant in spring or fall. Heathers thrive in sandy acid soil but can tolerate alkaline soils if enriched with rotted organic matter like compost or manure. Good for container displays, rockeries or fronts of borders.

PESTS AND DISEASES: Susceptible to powdery mildew.

DIANTHUS CARYOPHYLLUS

Commonly known as carnations or pinks, these plants produce clustered small purple, pink, red or white flowers, and are popular for adding colour to rockeries and borders.

FAMILY: *Caryophyllaceae*

FLOWERS: Bloom in clusters of around five spicily perfumed flowers, from spring to early summer.

LEAVES: Oppositely arranged, narrow, strap-like leaves that are typically grey or blue-green.

HABIT: Bushy herbaceous perennial that can grow up to a metre high.

PREFERRED ENVIRONMENT: Sun or partial shade, and minimal watering.

GROWING TIPS: Plant in spring, summer or fall. Neutral to alkaline soils.

PESTS AND DISEASES: Borers, mites, branch die back, rust and floral wilt.

FUCHSIA

With many species, varieties, cultivars and hybrids of *Fuchsia*, **the genus is easily recognisable by its pendulous flowers with red fused petals and prominent filaments.**

FAMILY: *Onagraceae*

FLOWERS: Teardrop shaped, with fused petals and sepals, often red, purple or yellowish, appearing summer to early fall.

LEAVES: Oppositely arranged, or in clusters, with serrated margins.

HABIT: Most *Fuchsias* thrive with little input, many species surviving tough winters. In cooler climates, some behave as herbaceous perennials – dying back in winter to regrow in spring. *Fuchsias* can be trailing or bushy and upright.

PREFERRED ENVIRONMENT: Most soils, including chalky ones, but they thrive in moisture-holding, loam-based compost.

GROWING TIPS: Great for pots and hanging baskets, *Fuchsias* should be fed with fertilizer. In spring, prune hardier types and pinch back tender varieties for second blooms.

PESTS AND DISEASES: Vulnerable to gall mite, various insects and leaf rot.

GERANIUM

Sometimes known as meadow cranesbill, these hardy or "true" *Geraniums* display small blue flowers through June and July, and will re-flower if deadheaded.

FAMILY: *Geraniaceae*

FLOWERS: Five-petalled, usually pale blue or violet with white veins, about 2 cm wide. Very attractive to butterflies and bees.

LEAVES: Deeply divided with seven to nine lobes, 7–15 cm width. Grows in a mound during spring.

HABIT: Herbaceous perennial. Flowers in a bushy growth pattern reaching up to 90 cm in height and spreading approximately 60 cm.

PREFERRED ENVIRONMENT: Moist but well-drained soil. Suitable for front or middle of a border. Can grow in either full sun or dappled shade.

GROWING TIPS: Plant and propagate in the spring.

PESTS AND DISEASES: Generally resilient, but can fall foul of vine weevils, capsid bugs and sawflies, and powdery mildew.

HYPERICUM FORRESTII

Related to St John's wort, Forrest St John's wort (named not for forest environments but to honour the plant's discoverer, Scottish botanist John Forrest) forms bushy clusters of bright yellow flowers.

FAMILY: *Hypericaceae*

FLOWERS: Blooms in summer, with saucer-shaped yellow petals, crowded with yellow stamens and prominent, thick yellow styles protruding from their centres.

LEAVES: Ovate, reddening in winter.

HABIT: Bushy and spreading, this semi-evergreen plant can grow 1.5 m in height and width.

PREFERRED ENVIRONMENT: Moist but well-drained soil. Full sun or partial shade.

GROWING TIPS: Plant in spring or fall. Propagate by seed sown in containers or semi-hardwood cuttings.

PESTS AND DISEASES: Susceptible to rust and honey fungus.

LOBELIA INFLATA

A native of North America, this wood-loving plant produces pale blue to violet flowers along tiny-haired stalks.

FAMILY: *Campanulaceae*

FLOWERS: Range from pale blue to white, or soft violet. Flowering midsummer to fall.

LEAVES: Oval, toothed, alternate.

HABIT: Up to 1 m tall, the plants will spill over the edges of a hanging basket.

PREFERRED ENVIRONMENT: Thrives in wet, moist soils, in full sun or partial shade.

GROWING TIPS: Plant in spring. Ideal for pond edges or baskets.

PESTS AND DISEASES: Vulnerable to slugs and snails, crown rot and wilting.

LYSIMACHIA PUNCTATA

Commonly referred to as yellow loosestrife, this plant is known for its spires of yellow flowers. Native to Turkey and Southern Europe, it forms in clumps and naturally thrives along wet coasts, ditches and roadsides.

FAMILY: *Primulaceae*

FLOWERS: Yellow star-shaped flowers with orange-red centres, arranged in tall spikes. Blooms in the summer.

LEAVES: Broad, light green leaves.

HABIT: A bushy herbaceous evergreen that typically grows to a height and spread of approximately 0.5–1 m. Often used as ground cover.

PREFERRED ENVIRONMENT: Well-drained soil in full sun or partial shade, and benefits from moist conditions.

GROWING TIPS: Plant in spring or summer. Cut back or remove faded flowers to make the plant look tidier in late season.

PESTS AND DISEASES: Vulnerable to slugs and snails.

MYOSOTIS SCORPIOIDES

Commonly known as forget-me-nots, these plants can be grown as perennials or biennials, their blue flowers among the smallest of garden plants. Native to wet habitats like riversides and ditches, they can survive being submerged in water.

FAMILY: *Boraginaceae*

FLOWERS: Small flowers up to 12 mm wide, with five blue petals and a yellow centre, blooming from spring to early summer.

LEAVES: Alternate arrangements of linear to oblong, grey-green leaves with tiny hairs, giving them a rough texture.

HABIT: Low growing with a creeping habit.

PREFERRED ENVIRONMENT: Damp, marshy ground and thrives in shade.

GROWING TIPS: Plant in spring or summer alongside other shade-lovers like *Hostas* to create attractive displays.

PESTS AND DISEASES: Susceptible to downy and powdery mildew.

NARCISSUS

Commonly known as daffodils, *Narcissus* grow from spring flowering bulbs and are easy to care for. They come in many species and hybrids though they all share a similar appearance: yellow or white flower heads at the end of a stalk, featuring a central trumpet-shaped structure.

FAMILY: *Amaryllidaceae*

FLOWERS: Typically, six tepals (petal-like features) surrounding a trumpet or bell-shaped structure. Usually yellow or white flower heads, but some garden varieties are orange or even pink.

LEAVES: Long green sheath-like leaves, which turn floppy after the plant has flowered.

HABIT: Suitable for borders, daffodils grow to about 30 cm in height.

PREFERRED ENVIRONMENT: Daffodils like full sun for at least 6 hours a day, and well-drained soil.

GROWING TIPS: Plant bulbs in September. Cut foliage once it begins yellowing.

PESTS AND DISEASES: Can be affected by yellow stripe virus.

PRIMULA VERIS

Commonly known as cowslips, these plants are herbaceous perennials bearing clusters of yellow flowers that appear in early spring. Each stem supports a group of 10–30 flowers.

FAMILY: *Primulaceae*

FLOWERS: Five-petalled, buttercup-yellow with single orange dashes at the centre.

LEAVES: Basal rosettes up to around 15 cm long.

HABIT: Evergreen or semi-evergreen.

PREFERRED ENVIRONMENT: Ideally moist soil with part shade.

GROWING TIPS: Plant in late summer or fall. Leave to self-seed after flowering. Enhance soil fertility by adding compost each year or apply well-rotted manure.

PESTS AND DISEASES: Watch out for vine weevil and leaf spot.

ROSA GALLICA

Rosa gallica is one of the first roses cultivated in Europe, notable for its red, purple or dark pink flowers.

FAMILY: *Rosaceae*

FLOWERS: Blooms in summer, with five petals in clusters of between one and four.

LEAVES: Pinnately compound, three to seven blue-green leaflets.

HABIT: Shrubby and compact.

PREFERRED ENVIRONMENT: Full sun and humus-rich, moist but well-drained soil.

GROWING TIPS: Plant in spring or summer. Use a balanced fertilizer and apply mulch in late winter or early spring.

PESTS AND DISEASES: Susceptible to aphids and other small insects.

SALVIA YANGII

Salvia "Blue Spire", also known as *Perovskia* and Russian sage, is a small leafy plant known for its striking panicles of blue flowers on white stems. This upright, densely forming plant adds a touch of elegance to summer gardens.

FAMILY: *Lamiaceae*

FLOWERS: Plumes of violet-blue on stems reaching up to 1.5 m, with a lifespan of about five years.

LEAVES: Grey-green.

HABIT: Upright growth forming dense blooms.

PREFERRED ENVIRONMENT: Poor but well-drained soil in full sun.

GROWING TIPS: Plant in late spring or early summer. Propagate by softwood cuttings in late spring or semi-ripe cuttings in summer.

PESTS AND DISEASES: Largely untroubled by pests, but diseases include wilt, foot and root rot, and powdery mildew.

TANACETUM VULGARE

Tanacetum vulgare, commonly known as tansy, is easily recognized by its bright yellow buttons of flowers. Often found growing wild near water or by roadsides and verges, this plant is popular in companion planting, combining well with vegetables because its scent repels some insects.

FAMILY: *Asteraceae*

FLOWERS: The aromatic, flat-topped yellow flowers sprout in clusters in summer through to fall. The flower heads are tightly packed with spirally arranged disc florets.

LEAVES: The compound leaves are alternately arranged and thinly divided into segments.

HABIT: Spreads via rhizomes.

PREFERRED ENVIRONMENT: At least 6 hours of sunlight per day. Once established, it becomes drought tolerant and benefits the soil by accumulating and adding potassium.

GROWING TIPS: Seeds can be sown directly into the ground in fall and should be worked well into the soil. In early spring, cut back close to the ground.

PESTS AND DISEASES: Spider mites can be problematic.

BEGONIA

Begonias are tender annuals which come in many varieties. Those with tuberous roots suit bedding schemes, while more fibrous rooted *Begonias* are perfect for hanging baskets and containers.

FAMILY: *Begoniaceae*

FLOWERS: Bright, glossy flowers often in shades of red or yellow, with densely arranged petals that form rosette-type clusters. They bloom from mid to late summer, often extending into fall as late as mid-October.

LEAVES: Leaves come in many shapes and are usually asymmetric.

HABIT: Up to 50 cm height and spread.

PREFERRED ENVIRONMENT: Full sun or partial shade.

GROWING TIPS: Plant outside following frost. If growing from seed, sow in early spring into well-drained moist soil or multipurpose compost.

PESTS AND DISEASES: Susceptible to whitefly and other insects as well as powdery mildew. Over- or under-watering can cause flower droop and leaf spots.

CALENDULA

Calendula are hardy annuals with daisy-like flowers, typically in bright shades of orange or yellow.

FAMILY: *Asteraceae*

FLOWERS: Many have bright yellow flowers consisting of a centre of disc florets, surrounded by comparatively long yellow ray florets. In common species like *C. officianalis*, the outer florets are so densely gathered they appear as a single unbroken entity. Blooms from summer through to first frosts.

LEAVES: Usually long, smooth and often hairless.

HABIT: Low-growing and bushy.

PREFERRED ENVIRONMENT: Most soils, including poorer and drier soils. Thrives in full sun but can tolerate shade.

GROWING TIPS: Seeds can be sown from March through spring. Plant out once established in summer. Avoid overly wet soils and deep shade.

PESTS AND DISEASES: Susceptible to aphids, thrips, whiteflies, powdery mildew, fungi and certain viruses.

CAMELLIA JAPONICA

Camellia japonica is a decorative plant known for its bounteous flowers of rosy pinks, snow whites and rich reds. With thousands of varieties, these *Camellias* are native to China and were later introduced to Japan.

FAMILY: *Theaceae*

FLOWERS: Usually single or double flowers appearing in spring, with interwoven petals and clustered petaloids and stamens. Flowers appear at the ends of branchlets, either solitary or in clusters.

LEAVES: Thick, dark leaves arranged alternately.

HABIT: Often upright, sometimes spreading to around 8 m.

PREFERRED ENVIRONMENT: Native to forest environments, it prefers shade and slightly acid, moist but well-drained soils.

GROWING TIPS: Best planted in fall or spring. Cuttings from semi-hardwood are a successful means of propagation.

PESTS AND DISEASES: Susceptible to aphids, scale insects, vine weevils, leaf rot, leaf blight and gall. Also prone to fungal diseases and injuries caused by high levels of salt in soils. Can rot in poorly drained soils.

CLARKIA

Popular garden annuals, *Clarkias* are ideal for beginners due to their simple cultivation and care. They encompass many species, most of which display lilac-coloured flowers from June through October.

FAMILY: *Onagraceae*

FLOWERS: Typically, four petals and four sepals, often light pink or white and occasionally streaked or spotted. Some species, such as *C. amoena*, have cup-shaped flower heads with petals almost fused; others, like *C. delicata*, have distinct, separate petals.

LEAVES: Small, simple leaves up to 10 cm long.

HABIT: If grown in large groups, produces profuse and vibrant displays.

PREFERRED ENVIRONMENT: Comfortable in most soils, from well-drained to moist. Full sun to partial shade. Ideal for borders or containers.

GROWING TIPS: Sow seeds in early June and water well during dry spells.

PESTS AND DISEASES: Susceptible to aphids, mealy bugs and scale insects.

COSMOS BIPINNATUS

Cosmos bipinnatus are much loved garden annuals, known for their tall stems that bear multicoloured clusters of flowers. When sown or planted in abundance, they create a stunning display of swaying colours.

FAMILY: *Asteraceae*

FLOWERS: Approximately 5 cm wide, with yellow disc florets at the centre, surrounded by eight purplish pink or white ray florets.

LEAVES: Finely threaded, feathery in appearance with linear pointed tips.

HABIT: Prone to wildflower-meadow-type clusters.

PREFERRED ENVIRONMENT: Half-hardy and frost intolerant. Prefers full sun but tolerates partial shade. Vulnerable to heavy rain, which can cause stems to break. Thrives in alkaline soils.

GROWING TIPS: Plant in the spring. Flowering season lengthened by deadheading, while self-seeding is promoted by leaving some seed heads to ripen.

PESTS AND DISEASES: Susceptible to aphids, slugs and grey moulds.

ESCHSCHOLZIA CALIFORNICA

Commonly known as the California poppy, this plant grows in perennial and annual forms, and produces cup-like flowers of luscious orange. Perfect for hot areas with poor soil.

FAMILY: *Papaveraceae*

FLOWERS: Solitary terminal flowers with silky petals, ranging from orange to yellow or red, which close at night. Blooms throughout summer.

LEAVES: Alternate, pale blue-green leaves.

HABIT: Often forms lush blankets of colour.

PREFERRED ENVIRONMENT: Full sun. In its native Californian environment and similarly warm areas, the plant will survive winter. In colder climates, it usually behaves as an annual, dying back in frost and cold weather. Drought tolerant and likes sandy, well-drained soils.

GROWING TIPS: Can be grown in pots or containers using all-purpose potting soils and compost.

PESTS AND DISEASES: Generally pest and disease free.

HELIANTHUS ANNUUS

The unmistakable sunflower boasts large yellow flower heads on tall, sturdy stems, which are smooth and tough but flexible enough to sway in the breeze. Ideal for large pots.

FAMILY: *Asteraceae*

FLOWERS: The plant's iconic yellow petals are actually ray florets, with the disc florets spirally arranged in the centre of the flower head.

LEAVES: Triangular to oval, serrated and bristly in texture.

HABIT: Heights of up to 3 m.

PREFERRED ENVIRONMENT: Sunflowers like well-drained, nutrient-rich soils, benefiting from the addition of well-rotted manure or compost.

GROWING TIPS: Sow from seed in the spring. Plant out when frost has passed and the soil is warming up.

PESTS AND DISEASES: Vulnerable to many insect predators, fungal diseases, downy mildew and the parasitic plant *Orobanche*.

IPOMOEA CAIRICA

A species of the morning glory genus, this showy plant produces purple to white flowers which grow quickly, making it well liked by gardeners who may wish to cover unsightly walls or fences.

FAMILY: *Convolvulaceae*

FLOWERS: Lavender coloured, funnel-shaped or tubular, with the petals lending a disc-like appearance. Appears singly or in clusters. Blooms most abundantly in spring and summer.

LEAVES: Alternate oval to circular leaves, divided into segments, reaching up to 9 cm in width.

HABIT: A climber, vining and herbaceous. *I. cairica* can also be used as ground cover.

PREFERRED ENVIRONMENT: Warm environments with little to no frost.

GROWING TIPS: If growing from seed, thin out seedlings about 45 cm apart once they emerge.

PESTS AND DISEASES: Susceptible to aphids, whitefly, weevils and moths.

LOBULARIA MARITIMA

This Mediterranean *Alyssum* is a member of the mustard family known for attracting beneficial insects. It is occasionally grown as a short-lived perennial and is often used as a bedding plant due to its profuse flowering.

FAMILY: *Brassicaceae*

FLOWERS: Tiny white flowers, about 5 mm in diameter, arranged densely along the stems, which bloom all summer.

LEAVES: Alternate, smooth leaves 1–4 cm in length and 3–5 mm wide.

HABIT: Low-growing, *L. maritima* can thrive in wall cracks and is effective for covering unsightly spaces.

PREFERRED ENVIRONMENT: Naturally adapted to sand and dunes, so likes free-draining acid soils. Heat and drought resistant but can benefit from shade in hotter climates.

GROWING TIPS: Plant in early spring. Deadheading encourages more blooms.

PESTS AND DISEASES: Susceptible to rots, mould and mildew.

NIGELLA DAMASCENA

Often called love-in-a-mist, *Nigella damascena* is a member of the buttercup family. Its blue flowers are almost buried in masses of lace-like structures, spread like spiny leaves.

FAMILY: *Ranunculaceae*

FLOWERS: Saucer shaped, usually blue, with 5–25 oval to triangular sepals, blooming throughout the summer.

LEAVES: Pinnately divided, thread-like leaves.

HABIT: Upright and bushy.

PREFERRED ENVIRONMENT: Well-drained soil in full sun, preferably alkaline or neutral, and benefits from a sheltered position.

GROWING TIPS: If propagating by seed, sow mid-spring or fall where you want the plants to grow. Fall-sown plants may need a cloche or cold frame for protection, depending on the climate.

PESTS AND DISEASES: Generally free of both.

OSTEOSPERMUM

Commonly known as African daisy, *Osteospermum* originates from Southern Africa and the Arabian peninsula. These hardy annuals thrive in full sun and warm summer temperatures.

FAMILY: *Asteraceae*

FLOWERS: Central disc florets surrounded by crowded orange, purple or white ray florets, blooming in late spring.

LEAVES: Mostly green, occasionally variegated.

HABIT: Low growing and plentiful.

PREFERRED ENVIRONMENT: Full sun and well-drained soils, but sheltered from wind. Ideally suited to pots on windowsills or patios.

GROWING TIPS: Plant in the spring. Water frequently.

PESTS AND DISEASES: Prone to aphids.

PELARGONIUM HORTORUM

Commonly known as zonal geranium, *P. hortorum* is a hybrid of two species in the genus and is divided into many cultivars, with *Pelargonium × hortorum* L. H. Bailey being the most popular.

FAMILY: *Geraniaceae*

FLOWERS: Single or double flowers with five petals. Typically pink, but other colours have been developed.

LEAVES: Circular with a slit-like division at the rear, and leaf margins.

HABIT: Profuse flowering.

PREFERRED ENVIRONMENT: Full sun with regular watering in the morning, afternoon and evening.

GROWING TIPS: Plant in the spring. Ideal for containers and ample space in soils.

PESTS AND DISEASES: Susceptible to whitefly and root rot.

TAGETES ERECTA

The yellow flowers of *Tagetes erecta*, commonly known as African or Aztec marigolds, are a familiar sight in parks and gardens. These marigolds are native to Mexico.

FAMILY: *Asteraceae*

FLOWERS: Pom-pom-like blooms, solitary or grouped inflorescences appearing in summer.

LEAVES: Pinnate lanceolate leaves with 11–17 leaflets. Basal leaves are opposite, while those higher on the stem are alternate, reaching up to 20 cm long.

HABIT: Herbaceous, growing up to approximately 110 cm tall.

PREFERRED ENVIRONMENT: Full sun and adapts well to most soil types, especially moist loam or sandy.

GROWING TIPS: Plant in the spring. May need staking and support as tall enough to blow over.

PESTS AND DISEASES: Vulnerable to beetles, spider mites, molluscs and fungal infection, particularly when overwatered or foliage becomes wet late in the evening or night.

VIOLA WITTROCKIANA

Violas (or pansies) come in many different colours, their flowers composed of three fragile petals. Easy to care for, pansies are a favourite among annuals.

FAMILY: *Violaceae*

FLOWERS: Two overlapping petals, two adjacent, with a fifth below resembling a beard. Will bloom all summer, often continuing into fall.

LEAVES: Heart-shaped, initially bronze coloured turning purple, red or orange in fall.

HABIT: Grows to a height and spread of approximately 15–30 cm.

PREFERRED ENVIRONMENT: Full sun or partial shade in fertile soil. Prefers cool weather.

GROWING TIPS: Plant in late spring or summer. As with many tender annuals, water by pouring to roots rather than spraying, which can cause fungal diseases.

PESTS AND DISEASES: Susceptible to aphids and molluscs, mildews, cucumber mosaic virus and stem rot.

ZINNIA

Zinnias are colourful bedding plants native to Mexico, thriving in hot conditions, and celebrated for their extensive flowering seasons.

FAMILY: *Asteraceae*

FLOWERS: Varieties include single or disc-like flowers and those with profuse dome-shaped petals.

LEAVES: Oppositely arranged and typically without stalks (sessile).

HABIT: Tend to be upright, but some species have trailing stems.

PREFERRED ENVIRONMENT: Full sun and well-drained soil.

GROWING TIPS: If sowing from seed, sow indoors in free-draining compost from February to April, transplanting once first true leaves appears. Sow outdoors into soil in May. Liquid feed and regular flower removal ensures continuous blooming.

PESTS AND DISEASES: Susceptible to leaf spot, mould and powdery mildew.

AQUILEGIA

Aquilegias, commonly known as columbine or granny's bonnet, are typically annuals, but can be grown as biennials if sown mid to late summer. They flower in spring and self-seed, ensuring future displays.

FAMILY: *Ranunculaceae*

FLOWERS: *Aquilegias* flower on stalks of up to around 60 cm in height, in colours ranging from rich reds and yellows to creamy whites, blues or soft pinks. The flowers often have elongated face-like shapes and spurred petals.

LEAVES: Pale green or grey leaves arranged in rosettes.

HABIT: Forms in clumps.

PREFERRED ENVIRONMENT: Most are suited to alpine-like climates, tolerating both sun or shade, and most soils – but preferably not too wet or dry.

GROWING TIPS: While *Aquilegias* do not require much watering, a generous soak after cutting back post-flowering will promote substantial new foliage.

PESTS AND DISEASES: Susceptible to powdery mildew in overly dry conditions. Watch out for specific pests like midges and sawflies.

DIPSACUS FULLONUM

Commonly known as teasel, this plant often grows by riversides and is recognized by its fuzzy flower heads. These bristly-tipped biennials are regularly cultivated on nature reserves, not least because their seeds form important food sources for birds in winter.

FAMILY: *Caprifoliaceae*

FLOWERS: Forming at the heads of their prickly stems, the flowers are usually purplish, with hundreds of them compacted into oval-like shapes.

LEAVES: Prickly, oppositely arranged rosettes.

HABIT: Tall and upright, making them ideal for the back of a border.

PREFERRED ENVIRONMENT: Full sun to partial shade in moist or well-drained soil.

GROWING TIPS: Can be sown in spring to flower the following summer.

PESTS AND DISEASES: Relatively pest-resistant. Even aphids that occasionally appear are consumed by the birds and ladybirds they attract.

ECHIUM VULGARE

E. vulgare, commonly known as viper's bugloss or spotted stems, is native to Europe and thrives in dry, sandy environments. The roots were traditionally used as remedies for snake bites. It is toxic to cows and horses.

FAMILY: *Boraginaceae*

FLOWERS: Small, funnel-shaped flowers that turn blue as they mature, growing on branches in long spikes. They feature protruding stamens and bloom in summer.

LEAVES: Bluish-green, spiky rosettes.

HABIT: Strong and upright.

PREFERRED ENVIRONMENT: Chalky or poor soils and unimproved grassland, thriving in dry patches with full sun.

GROWING TIPS: Grow from seed after frost has passed in spring where you want the plants to grow, as transplanting can damage long taproots. No feeding required, but occasional watering helps sustain nectar production.

PESTS AND DISEASES: Generally pest-free.

LUNARIA ANNUA

Lunaria annua, **or common honesty, is a relative of cabbages and mustard, bearing purplish, pink or violet flowers that grow at the end of its stems.**

FAMILY: *Brassicaceae*

FLOWERS: Clusters of four- or five-petalled flowers bloom in spring and summer. The flowers are followed by thin, oval, papery seed packets called "siliques" which are translucent green to light brown, and often used in floral arrangements.

LEAVES: Large rough leaves, with the lower ones being stalked.

HABIT: Grows up to 90 cm, making it suitable for the back of a border.

PREFERRED ENVIRONMENT: Fertile, slightly alkaline, well-drained but moist soils.

GROWING TIPS: Sow from seeds in summer, or plant in the fall, for flowering the following spring.

PESTS AND DISEASES: Susceptible to fungal diseases and club root.

OENOTHERA BIENNIS

Commonly called evening primrose, this biennial North American native opens its flowers in the evening, as the name suggests.

FAMILY: *Onagraceae*

FLOWERS: Bow-shaped yellow flowers appear in groups at the tips of the stems, blooming most abundantly in late summer.

LEAVES: In the first year, the lanceolate leaves form in rosettes, spiralling in the second.

HABIT: The plant typically begins its first year in a low-spreading form, but in its second year, the woody stems can grow up to 1.6 m tall in some climates.

PREFERRED ENVIRONMENT: Bright conditions, but not direct sun. Moist but well-drained soils.

GROWING TIPS: Due to its potential height, position towards the middle or back of a border.

PESTS AND DISEASES: Susceptible to slugs and snails. Root rot can be an issue in overly moist or wet soils.

CHAPTER THREE

LANDSCAPING IDEAS

In this chapter, we look at some of the different types of garden you might create, depending on your interests, environment and the space you have available.

We'll explore wildlife, cottage, rockery, herb, kitchen and ornamental gardens, but keep in mind that your garden doesn't have to fit neatly into one category and can be a combination of different ideas. After all, gardening is a journey of experimentation and discovery, allowing you to find what thrives in your unique climate and environment.

WILDLIFE GARDEN

Wildlife gardens boost biodiversity, allowing you to enjoy floral colour while helping our fluttering friends and buzzing companions!

The main pollinators you will attract are butterflies and bees. A garden full of nectar-rich, flat or bowl-shaped flowers like *Asters*, daisies and *Zinnias* will also attract many other beneficial insects like beetles, hoverflies and wasps.

Birds love nesting in *Berberis*, box and hawthorn hedges, which provide them with fruits from late summer through fall. They are also attracted to food provided on bird tables and bird feeders. Typically hanging contraptions, feeders are increasingly made of eco-friendly materials like zinc alloy and recyclable polycarbonate, which will not weaken in sunlight, and hold bird food like suet balls, nuts and seeds. They can be height-adjusted and are often designed to attract birds of different sizes.

Water features are great for wildlife. If you lack space for a pond, consider installing a small bird bath. A bird bath is best placed out of direct sun to avoid the water drying, and is valuable in both summer and winter, especially when natural sources may have frozen. Ensure the bath has shallow and sloping sides so wildlife do not get stuck and drown. Equally, make sure the water is not too deep, or smaller birds may be unable to breathe. Position the bath away from hedges or foliage where predators could hide, and elevate it to reduce the risk of predation.

To make your own bird bath, start with a terracotta plant pot and saucer. Place the pot upside down and attach the saucer to its base using waterproof glue. Leave it for 24 hours to ensure the glue dries. To reduce the risk of drowning, add stones to enable birds and bees to perch safely. You can also use fountains to attract wildlife, typically made of stone or stainless steel and found at most garden centres.

Bees prefer open flowers because the central parts are easier to access. They see purple more clearly than any other colour, making plants like *Alliums*, lavender and purple toadflax worthy additions to a wildlife garden.

Other bee-attracting plants include *Asters* and borage, whose bright-blue flowers and large stores of nectar make them irresistible, along with mints and meadow cranesbill, red clover, rosemary, *Stachys byzantina* ("lamb's ears") with soft, silvery foliage and spike-like stems of small purple flowers, and teasel. *Monarda*, with jazzy red flowers, is so beloved of bees that its common name is "bee balm".

Winter honeysuckle and winter clematis can sustain bees out of season (in some climates, bees might visit from late February until as late as November).

A small spot may be perfect for a "wildlife patch", unmown and sown with wildflower seeds. Full sun is best, though many wildflower mixes contain seeds suitable for light shade.

Scattering seeds (or "broadcasting") is a popular technique for achieving a natural effect. Most wildflowers thrive in poor soils of the type common in meadows, but a few prefer damp soils and are often seen near water. If you are planting common fleabane, cuckoo flower, purple loosestrife, ragged robin or snake's head fritillary, an ideal place would be the edge of a small pond, or a shaded part of the garden exposed to moisture.

An often-overlooked feature of great benefit to wildlife is the log pile, which provides excellent habitats for reptiles, amphibians and even some small birds.

There are no hard rules about how to create your wildlife garden, but whichever plants you choose, and however you arrange them, both you and nature will reap the rewards.

GREEN FINGERS:

THREE WILDLIFE GARDENING TIPS

1. Try to use native plants and identify what thrives locally by visiting local green spaces and, if possible, other gardens. The wildlife in your area has evolved to consume or interact with native plants, so growing these plants will give your garden a good chance of attracting them.

2. Shade creates corridors for wildlife to travel through undetected by predators.

3. Be patient: some plants take years to mature. For example, you're unlikely to see a song thrush feeding on ivy berries for at least five years.

THREE POPULAR WILDLIFE GARDEN PLANTS

Butterfly bush (*Buddleja davidii*)

Buddleja is a deciduous shrub native to East Asia which can spread to around 4.5 m. Its purple and lilac blooms cluster on cone-shaped spikes during the summer.

Buddleja is beloved by butterflies – hence its nickname "butterfly bush" – and tolerates conditions ranging from full sun to shade, and adapts well to most soils.

To prevent early, excessive flowering, *Buddleja* should be pruned in late April, encouraging blooms in August, which aligns with peak butterfly season. The plant can also be propagated by hardwood cuttings and typically flowers for around one month.

Buddleja davidii can be targeted by aphids, capsid bugs, caterpillars, various moths, spider mites and weevils. It is also susceptible to honey fungus and fungal leaf spot.

Foxglove (*Digitalis purpurea*)

Digitalis purpurea, commonly known as foxglove, grows to around 2 m tall and is a food source for long-tongued pollinators like butterflies and bees. The thimble-like flowers, arranged on long stems, are typically purple or pink, with some varieties white or yellow.

The Latin name, *Digitalis purpurea*, refers to the plant's purple colour and its finger-shaped flowers ("*digitalis*" meaning fingers). Legend has it that foxes wore them around their paws to muffle the sound of their approach to prey – hence the name foxgloves.

The main difference between wild and cultivated foxgloves is that the wild varieties display blossoms on only one side of the stem.

Foxgloves thrive in acid, humus-rich soils that are neither too wet nor too dry. They are light-loving plants, ideal for dappled sun, and are rarely found in full shade.

These perennials are best planted in fall or spring, whether in borders or containers. They are hardy and survive most winters.

Foxgloves are toxic so remember to wear gloves when handling the plants or seeds.

Lavender (*Lavandula*)

A beloved English wildflower, lavender also blossoms in temperate North American climates like Washington and Oregon states, and even sunny California. The narrow foliage is silvery grey, while purple, lilac, violet or blue flowers are arranged in whorls on stems around 1 m tall.

A hardy perennial, lavender is aromatic, drought tolerant and easy to care for. It suits both border or container planting and is generally best pruned late summer to early fall, after flowering. It is ideal for propagation by cuttings: simply pinch off non-flowered shoots, dip cut edges into rooting hormone, and insert around the rim of a pot filled with grit-rich compost. Water the cuttings, cover with polythene and keep them in a warm, shady environment for four to six weeks (until flowering), then pot.

Lavender has few pests or diseases, making it a popular choice for attracting bees, butterflies and moths.

COTTAGE GARDEN

Cottage gardens are known for their informal and natural appearances, and with a few thoughtful steps, you can create a garden with a feel of the rural – even in the middle of town!

To achieve this look, consider a mix of planting and sowing. Alongside ready-potted plants from nurseries or garden centres, you will find a wide range of suitable seed mixtures on the market. When planning your garden, check the heights your plants will grow to on the seed packet, and remember it is best to place taller plants at the rear of any arrangement to avoid blocking out sunlight for the smaller ones.

One popular feature of cottage gardens is the floral border, which offers structure while still being free-flowing. It is often the first thing visitors notice, so it's worth planning how you want your border to look. Choose an open, sunny side of the garden with free-draining soil, and spread a 70-mm layer of well-rotted compost, which worms and micro-organisms will dig in. The border could surround a lawn, a path or maybe a wildflower plot. Some good cottage garden border plants include *Aquilegias* (colourful and easy to maintain perennials), *Dianthus* (low-growing pink and purple perennials that look great at the front of a border), lavender and tulips, which add a rich mixture of purples and reds, and buttercups to bring a splash of yellow. *Phlox* is excellent to fill in gaps, creating carpets of delicate pink and violet when planted densely.

Wild poppies are a classic choice for cottage gardens. From traditional red field poppies (*Papaver rhoeas*), to the beguiling yellows of Welsh poppy (*Papaver cambricum*) and the California poppy (*Eschscholzia californica*), these herbaceous favourites are best scattered in thin drifts of seeds.

Densely planted herbaceous perennials and plants with large, long petals work best, such as peonies and English roses. Hollyhocks and ox-eye daisies create a charming, informal look when planted in uneven rows, while the vibrant spikes of lupins add splashes of colour. A curving border makes smaller spaces look larger, while less bushy plants like mountain fleece add vertical appeal. Purple toadflax (*Linaria purpurea*), a herbaceous perennial similar to lavender but shorter, offers breeze-ruffled columns of purple racemes that attract some butterfly caterpillars. For shaded areas, plants like ferns, spurges and *Hostas* thrive and look stunning in borders.

Some gardeners combine ground-planted flowers with flowerpots on circular stepping stones for a less formal structure, adding gnomes and other ornaments in random spots. Stone pots ensure a rustic look, their earthy colours complemented by plants like *Astrantia major* (with delicate umbrellas of sparkling white flowers), and bright-flowered varieties like fountain grass (*Pennisetum setaceum*), which features pom-poms of purple flowers that fade to beige in fall, and *Gerberas*, from the *Aster* family, which present masses of multicoloured, dainty flowers – a nice contrast to the white or grey of a stone pot.

Smaller plants that complement a cottage garden include *Campanula*, catmint, *Geums* and *Geraniums*.

This style of garden will reward the senses and provide much aesthetic appeal, especially in spring and summer. With a bit of planning and seasonal care, you can create a bounteously floral cottage garden for you and all your garden guests to enjoy.

GREEN FINGERS:

THREE COTTAGE GARDEN TIPS

1. Create a rounded feel. Incorporate circular flower beds and planting, features like stone balls and pebbles in rounded patterns.

2. Embrace a colourful mix. Go for a jumble of colours, intermingling blue and red, purple and yellow flowers.

3. Choose cosy, vintage furniture. Add a homely feel by including a wooden gate rather than metal and a bench rather than deckchairs.

THREE POPULAR COTTAGE GARDEN PLANTS

Hollyhock (*Alcea rosea*)

Hollyhocks are a quintessential cottage garden plant, flowering throughout summer through to early fall, and delighting garden visitors with their glossy colours. The flowers, which can reach 12 cm in diameter, range from vivid purples to luscious reds and pinks.

Generally biennial, hollyhocks are profusely self-sowing, giving the impression of perennial habits. They should be planted in spring or fall, and if propagating from seed, sown in early spring directly where you want them to grow.

Pests and diseases to watch out for include slugs and snails, and rust fungus, though many commercial varieties are rust-resistant. Disease primarily targets the leaves.

Due to their height – reaching up to 8 m – hollyhocks are best planted at the backs of borders, with no pruning needed.

Honeysuckle (*Lonicera*)

Tumbling over garden walls, honeysuckles are dazzling plants with vibrant colours, blooming throughout summer and early fall. The tubular flowers are yellow and red, attracting butterflies and long-tongued bees. While some species, like *L. periclymenum*, have a climbing habit, others, such as *L. ligustrina*, have a shrubby aspect.

These densely blooming, bright-berried plants (the red fruits can be slightly poisonous, but also attract wildlife) are good for covering unattractive walls or overgrown areas. Their natural habitats are woods and shady corners, and they are native to much of North Africa, Europe and the Caucasus, growing as far north as Finland. Their growing conditions are not confined to full sun and they will grow in both acidic or alkaline soils provided the soil is well-drained. Being deciduous, they should be pruned after flowering to promote healthy growth.

Rudbeckia

A member of the daisy (*Asteraceae*) family, the vibrant *Rudbeckia* is a North American native known for its striking yellow flowers. Blooms can range from 25 cm to 1 m in height, appearing through summer and early fall. As the season ends, the seed heads provide food for birds, and the flowers can last over a week in vases.

The most popular variety is *R. hirta*, known as "black-eyed Susan" an annual or short-lived perennial.

The large lanceolate leaves are narrow and toothed, while the flowers are composed of star-shaped yellow ray florets, with a central dark dome of disc florets.

Black-eyed Susan is often planted in large groups, creating bright and cheerful displays in the garden.

ROCKERY

Rockeries provide striking visual displays, while assisting biodiversity by providing habitats for invertebrates. The alpine plants most suited to them are often sources of nectar for pollinators.

To start, mark out the area intended for the rockery with pegs and string, and consider placing landscaping fabric on the ground to impede potential weeds. Rockeries do best in full sun, so choose your location accordingly. Weeds should be removed to avoid them disrupting the soil. As for the rocks themselves, you may need to source them from a location like a reclamation yard. The largest rocks, or "keystones", may need moving with a crowbar, and tilting backwards for a natural look. These rocks should be buried up to a third of their depth, and surrounded by smaller rocks and stones.

Most plants suited for rockeries prefer full sun, and dislike shade or damp. Many gardeners prioritize alpines and wildflowers, such as *Aubrieta*, *Campanula*, red star (*Rhodohypoxis baurii*) and succulents like *Sedums*. Depending on how dry and warm your climate is, cacti may also make good choices in a rockery.

Plants should be positioned in "pockets" between rocks, with compost applied firmly over roots. A layer of grit or gravel will aid drainage and reduce the chances of weeds. Alpines generally do well in a compost mix of loam, horticultural grit, and coir or leaf mould.

Whether you choose just a small patch of your garden, or the whole space, a rockery can be a relaxing place to sit and contemplate the beauty of nature. It offers a unique combination of the sturdiness of stone with the delicate charm of floral colour, bringing a touch of alpine landscape to your own backyard.

THREE ROCKERY TIPS

1. Experiment with different plant shapes to add variety. Succulents are great as they often vary in appearance even within species.

2. Bright-coloured flowers like pasque-flowers and gentians add visual depth.

3. Position your rockery away from trees or high shrubs to avoid unwanted shadows.

THREE POPULAR ROCKERY PLANTS

House leek (*Sempervivum*)

House leeks are succulent perennials that are part of the *Crassulaceae* or "stonecrop" family. These highly distinctive plants are ideal for rockery planting due to their unique leafy structures and squat habits, springing up in cracks and pockets of soil like small spiky stars.

Sometimes mistaken for flower heads, the leaf rosettes are often coloured scarlet red or shades of green and yellow. The rosettes send out stolons (runners) on which young plantlets called offsets are produced, and in the right conditions spread quickly – hence the name *Sempervivum*, meaning "forever alive" in Latin.

House leeks thrive in crevices, stone troughs, between house bricks, or in otherwise inhospitable parts of a garden, provided they have well-drained soil. These unusual plants look stunning when arranged in geometric and ornamental patterns.

Mossy saxifrage
(*Saxifraga bryoides*)

These perennial alpines, thriving in the Arctic tundra and high-altitude mountain ranges of the northern hemisphere, are small but hardy plants that create dense cushions of colour in the winter or early spring months.

The solitary flowers occur in such profuse blooms that it can look as though they grow in clusters, with petals coloured white to creamy, or white with purplish tinges around their edges and thinly veined across their surfaces. The leaves curl up in winter to conserve energy.

Mossy saxifrage prefers well-drained and gritty soil, but can become detached from its roots in excessively damp conditions.

Thyme
(*Thymus vulgaris*)

A low-growing, purple-flowered herb from the mint family, thyme forms carpets of shrub-like growth ideal for filling small pockets between rocks. This alpine perennial prefers free-draining soil and full sun, with its nectar-rich flowers attracting beneficial insects like bees throughout the early summer.

The plant's tight-packed blooms combine well in displays with other small-flowered alpines, and its grey-green foliage is evergreen. Propagation by cuttings is popular, and like most herbs, the species has a delicious peppery taste when crushed.

HERB GARDEN

Herbs do best in sunny, sheltered spots, and while a smattering may complement any garden, it is possible to devote an entire garden to their cultivation. Although herb gardens require close care, the effort is well worth it.

Start by considering the kind of environment your herbs will be growing in. To keep things simple, it is easiest to grow herbs with similar requirements together. For instance, Mediterranean herbs, like oregano, rosemary, sage and thyme, prefer full sun but poor soil, benefiting from the addition of horticultural grit. In contrast, herbs from the Caucasus or Western Europe, like chervil, lavender, mint, parsley, sage and sorrel, benefit from some shade, and make excellent edging plants.

Herbs that thrive in moist soil and may bolt (quickly run to seed) in strong sunlight include basil, coriander, dill and purslane, and should be sown in small quantities and harvested frequently.

To organize your garden, consider delineating sections of herbs by pebbles, bricks, bark chippings or gravel, arranged in cartwheel or chessboard layouts.

Herbs can be grown in herb patches in soil, in rockeries or raised beds where you can determine the soil composition. For best results, many are sown firstly in indoor containers on windowsills at any time of year, before being pricked out and hardened off in the milder or warmer months. Some herbs are not frost-hardy and benefit from being grown in containers so they can be moved indoors during winter. Herbs in this category include African blue basil, lemongrass and lemon verbena. When growing herbs in pots, place crocks at the base, and add a peat-free compost together with some horticultural grit or perlite to aid drainage.

Ideally, position your herb garden near a seating area to benefit from their delightful fragrances. The herbs might be sown into the soil as seed, or propagated by semi-ripe cuttings in late summer or early fall.

Many herbs produce attractive flowers. A herb patch looks good with contrasting floral and foliar colours: dark-leaved herbs work well alongside those with warm, golden leaves.

GREEN FINGERS:

THREE HERB GARDEN TIPS

1. To lighten clay soil for annual herbs, dig in well-rotted compost.

2. Fill raised beds with topsoil and horticultural grit. This aids drainage and adds nutrients.

3. Some herbs, like mint, die down in winter, so late fall is a good time to cut them to the ground. Others, like rosemary and sage, get straggly, so it's best to prune them in spring or after flowering.

FLORAL FAVOURITES:
THREE POPULAR HERBS

Dill (*Anethum graveolens*)

Dill, related to celery, originates from warm climates such as North Africa and Greece. It grows from a taproot, producing hollow stems and soft, feathery, finely divided leaves, about a millimetre thick that are arranged alternately around the base and at intervals along the stem in long, grassy protrusions.

The small white or yellow flowers form on umbels, with seeds in small dark pods.

Dill thrives in full sun and prefers well-drained, moist soils, though it is possible to cultivate dill on a windowsill with regular watering.

Dill's fragrant leaves are popular as culinary herbs when fresh or freeze-dried to flavour soups. An extract from the plant is used as "dill oil", an essential oil used for help with sleep and various complaints, while oil from dill seeds is used in soaps.

Basil (*Ocimum basilicum*)

Native to India, basil can be sown indoors at any time of year but should not be sown or transplanted outdoors in winter. Grow on a south-facing windowsill, or outside in freshly dug-over soil that's been watered the day before sowing. Basil needs around 6–8 hours of sunlight per day.

To sow in pots or trays, sprinkle seeds over seed-growing or multipurpose compost, cover with about 0.5 cm of compost, firm in and lightly water. Basil wilts if inadequately watered – some people water it twice daily.

Seedlings should appear within a week. Once they develop two pairs of true leaves (not early seed leaves which soon fade), thin out the weaker seedlings.

O. basilicum produces purple flowers which can be pinched out to ensure the plant's energies are concentrated on foliage.

Basil leaves make irresistible additions to curries, pasta dishes and stir-fries. They can also be frozen for future use and are a food source for various butterfly larvae.

Tarragon (*Artemisia dracunculus*)

Tarragon is a popular culinary herb native to Eurasia and North America, known for its lanceolate, glossy green leaves which add a distinct flavour to salads. A staple in French cuisine, the plant grows to around 1.5 m, thrives in poor soil, and is drought tolerant, making it an ideal low-maintenance herb for the time-pressed gardener!

Tarragon's flowers are arranged in groups of about 40 yellow florets, which are highly attractive to pollinating insects in late summer.

There are essentially two types of tarragon: French and Russian. French tarragon carries a richer taste with hints of aniseed, while Russian tarragon is milder. Both kinds prefer full sun and well-drained soils or large containers.

The species name *dracunculus* is owed to the plant's coiled roots.

KITCHEN GARDEN

A kitchen garden is usually a space separate from the main garden and can take the form of an allotment. It is possible to create one even in a small garden area. Here are some ways you might rustle up your own delicious kitchen garden.

The first consideration is location. Leafy green crops like broccoli, cabbage and kale grow in cool climates and tolerate shade, but many salad vegetables and fruits prefer sunny spots.

The soil should be well-drained and nutrient-rich. Weeds should be removed, and clumps of soil broken up. Adding topsoil or compost will further enrich the soil.

Popular kitchen garden plants include apples, blackberries, brassicas, carrots, celery, gooseberries, onions, peas, potatoes, raspberries and rhubarb.

While kitchen gardens are functional, they need not be devoid of ornament. Many culinary plants produce attractive flowers, such as delicate umbels of carrots, vibrant yellows of Jerusalem artichokes (a member of the sunflower family), and the purple tufts of global artichokes (*Cynara scolymus*). In winter, ornamental cabbages flower in rosettes of rich purples, bright reds and silky pinks. Non-culinary plants can also be dotted around edible ones.

GREEN FINGERS:
THREE KITCHEN GARDEN TIPS

1. Ensure easy access to water sources.

2. Erect fencing to keep out predators.

3. Combining flowers and vegetables can be beneficial, as the flowers can attract pests away from vegetables. This is known as "trap cropping", and the most well-known example is the growing of nasturtiums (*Tropaeolum polyphyllum*) as border plants to entice aphids from prize crops.

THREE POPULAR KITCHEN GARDEN PLANTS

Crab apple

With their gorgeous spring blossoms and small ornamental apples, these hardy trees, from the *Malus* genus, benefit wildlife and tolerate many conditions. They thrive in moist, well-drained soil in full sun or partial shade.

The apples themselves, which range from red to yellow, are only edible once turned into sauce or jellies.

Water young trees regularly during their first few years, apply mulches of well-rotted compost or manure in spring, and prune in late winter.

Gooseberry

Gooseberries are soft fruits which produce abundant edible crops each summer, often for up to 15 years per plant. Home-grown varieties are usually juicy and tasty, and are worthy additions to any kitchen garden.

These low-maintenance plants can be trained to fit specific spaces with appropriate pruning. Gooseberries can be bought as bare root plants during their dormant period in winter or early spring. A two-to-three-year-old plant with a 10–15 cm stem will make a healthy gooseberry bush.

Along with being delicious on their own, gooseberries make great jams, sauces and ingredients for pies.

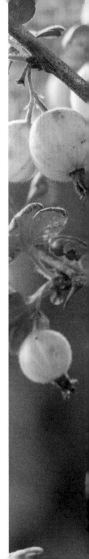

Potatoes

Potatoes must be grown from purposely produced seed potatoes, typically planted in the spring. As the plant grows, you should pile up soil around the stems – a process known as "earthing up" – to bury the developing tubers. They are often grown in rows, but if space is limited, potatoes grow just as well in containers. For winter harvesting, plant in large tubs in late summer, protected from frost in a greenhouse or a porch.

Regardless of how you cultivate your crop, you can look forward to abundant supplies and regular harvesting. Be warned: digging up spuds can be hard, back-ache-sparking work. Use a good, tough spade or a specially designed potato scoop. Remember to bend your knees, rather than your back, to avoid injury.

ORNAMENTAL GARDEN

Ornamental gardens showcase dazzling plants and features, in displays designed to be pleasing to the eye. They offer the perfect opportunity to incorporate water features or sculptures in ways that complement a horticultural display – blending contrasting colours or cultivating aquatic plants like lily pads in ponds. Showy plants such as Japanese maples, small and detailed flowers like *Asters* and chrysanthemums, elegant *Meillandine* roses which look striking in clay pots, and extravagant ornamental grasses are all prime candidates for an ornamental garden.

Three classic styles of ornamental horticulture are:

❊ **Traditional English garden:** profuse in flowers, with winding paths and whimsical features such as gnomes.

❊ **Japanese garden:** rocks and water combine with small trees, pruned shrubs and vertical plants like bamboo, bonsai, grasses and water lilies to lend a "Zen" calm.

❊ **Rose garden:** can range from formal to naturalistic themes, often featuring trellises, pergolas, obelisks and, if space permits, rose arches.

GREEN FINGERS:

THREE ORNAMENTAL GARDEN TIPS

1. Display flowers in "colour blocks" for a striking appearance.

2. Pale fences and boundaries will show off the vibrant colours of your plants.

3. Even a simple lawn can be ornamental – for example, you can mow the lawn into a circular shape, lending an illusion of more space.

THREE POPULAR ORNAMENTAL GARDEN PLANTS

Dahlias

The stunning colours and flower shapes of these tuberous, bushy plants are a delight to behold, and they are often the centrepieces of specialist public gardens.

Dahlias require shelter and full sun, fertile, moist but well-drained soil. Taller varieties should be staked to support their growth. As fall approaches, dig up the tubers and store them in frost-free environments like a shed or greenhouse, preferably in paper bags. Dahlias are not frost-hardy and need to be warm through the winter. In late spring, around May, replant the tubers once they have started to grow again to ensure a vibrant display for the new season.

Japanese maple (*Acer palmatum*)

The Japanese maple is a hardy small tree, greatly suited to pots, and a firm favourite for the ornamental garden. Its finely divided, filigree-style leaves provide delicious fall colours, often turning shades of orange, yellow, red or purple. Preferring shade and slightly acidic, sandy soils, it is adaptable but should be kept away from waterlogged areas.

Japanese maples flower in spring, and may be planted through the fall and winter, and given a good prune back in winter. Enrich planting holes with rotted organic matter. If growing in a pot, consider tree or shrub compost, or a generally loam-rich mix. Early to mid-spring planting is also possible, but most growers find this is most successful with the addition of slow-release fertilizer. In all cases, be sure to water well.

Tulips

Members of the lily (*Lilliaceae*) family, tulips are bulbiferous beauties, delighting the eye with cup-shaped flowers. The genus name *Tulipa* is thought to derive from the Persian word for turban, *tulipan*, which the flowers were said to resemble. The classic image of tulips is of deep-red flowers, but they can also be bright yellow, orange, white or rich purple.

Growing naturally on steppes and in mountainous areas, tulips have been cultivated for centuries, and even sparked a "tulip mania" in seventeenth-century Europe.

Tulips should be planted in the fall, to depths of at least three times the bulb's length, ends pointing upwards and spaced around 5 cm apart. They will flower in the spring and should be cut back in summer. Tulips thrive in full sun and are suited to both borders and pots. After blooming, bulbs need digging up and re-planting each year. Store them in a dark, dry and well-ventilated place such as a garage, basement or even a refrigerator.

FAREWELL

Hopefully, *The Little Book of Gardening* has sown the seeds of many gardening adventures and helped you realize a thriving garden is possible, even in small spaces. The trick is to understand and work with your environment.

For advice on choosing plants that suit your climate, pest control or irrigation, there are many sources to consult. Websites and online groups can be helpful, but nothing quite beats the expertise of experienced staff at nurseries and garden centres. As you progress through your horticultural exploits, you too will be able to share your knowledge, and help others embrace the joy of gardening.

It takes years to build up a wide knowledge of different plants, what works where, and the tools and management needed for specific situations. But far from being a reason to feel daunted, this is something to celebrate. Gardening is a labour of love, and each task – whether digging, planting, pruning or embarking on any of the many other pursuits we have looked at – adds to your stock of experience and knowledge.

We wish you well on your gardening journey. All that remains is to grasp the spade and secateurs and get gardening!

INDEX

African lily (*Agapanthus praecox*) 44

Annuals 18, 59–73

Begonias 59

Biennials 18, 74–8

Buttercups 91

Calendula 60

California poppy (*Eschscholzia californica*) 64, 91

Daffodils (*Narcissus*) 54

Dahlias 122

Daisies 81, 92

Evening primrose (*Oenothera biennis*) 78

Forget-me-nots (*Myosotis scorpioides*) 53

Fuchsia 48

Geranium 49, 92

Heather (*Calluna vulgaris*) 40, 46

Honeysuckle (*Lonicera*) 83, 97

Lavender (*Lavandula*) 40, 82, 89, 91, 106

Marigolds (*Tagetes erecta*) 71

Pansies (also known as Violas) (*Viola wittrockiana*) 72

Perennials 20, 44–58

Roses (*Rosa gallica*) 56, 92, 119

Russian sage (*Salvia yangii*) 57

Sunflowers (*Helianthus annuus*) 65

Tansy (*Tanacetum vulgare*) 58

Teasel (*Dipsacus fullonum*) 75, 82

Thrift (*Armeria maritima*) 45

Tulips 91, 124

Have you enjoyed this book?
If so, find us on Facebook at Summersdale Publishers
on Twitter/X at @Summersdale and on Instagram
and TikTok at @summersdalebooks and get in touch.
We'd love to hear from you!

www.summersdale.com